Science Songs

Move It! Work It!

A Song About Simple Machines

by Laura Purdie Salas
illustrated by Viviana Garofoli

Sing along to the tune of

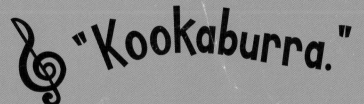
"Kookaburra."

Learn how simple machines make your life easier.

PICTURE WINDOW BOOKS
Minneapolis, Minnesota

Editor: Jill Kalz
Designer: Abbey Fitzgerald
Page Production: Melissa Kes
Art Director: Nathan Gassman
Editorial Director: Nick Healy
The illustrations in this book were created digitally.

Picture Window Books
151 Good Counsel Drive
P.O. Box 669
Mankato, MN 56002-0669
877-845-8392
www.picturewindowbooks.com

AUG 0 5 2009

Printed in the United States of America.

All books published by Picture Window Books
are manufactured with paper containing at least
10 percent post-consumer waste.

Library of Congress Cataloging-in-Publication Data
Salas, Laura Purdie.
Move it! Work it! : a song about simple machines / by Laura Purdie Salas ;
illustrated by Viviana Garofoli.
p. cm. – (Science Songs)
Includes index.
Summary: "Introduces the topic of simple machines through the familiar tune
"Kookaburra"–Summary provided by publisher.
ISBN 978-1-4048-5299-0 (library binding)
1. Simple machines–Juvenile literature 2. Simple machines–Songs and music.
3. Science–Songs and music. I. Garofoli, Viviana. II. Title. III. Title: Song about
simple machines.
TJ147.S25 2008
621.8–dc22   2008038442

Thanks to our advisers for their expertise, research, and advice:

Virg Debban, Secondary Science Teacher (ret.)
New Ulm (Minnesota) Public School ISD #88

Terry Flaherty, Ph.D., Professor of English
Minnesota State University, Mankato

Machines are things we use to make work easier. If you need to add a lot of big numbers, you might use a machine. If you need to dig a deep hole, you might use another machine.

When we think of machines, we often picture things that have many moving parts or use electricity. But there are six simple machines that help us do lots of work. They are the inclined plane, the wheel and axle, the lever, the wedge, the pulley, and the screw. These machines may look simple, but they make our lives easier.

Lifting the piano is a great big pain.

It will give your back a great big strain.

Roll, yes it will! Roll, up the hill!

Use an inclined plane.

4

An inclined plane is a surface that is sloped. It makes it easier to move heavy loads up or down. A loading ramp is one example of an inclined plane.

inclined plane

Do you ride a bike to your friend's each day?

Pedal place to place without delay?

Go, wheel and axle! Go, wheel and axle!

Take me far away.

wheel

axle

A wheel and axle is made of one or more wheels attached to a bar. It helps move things. Cars and Ferris wheels have wheels and axles.

7

When you row a rowboat on the lake,

Pairs of wooden oars are what you take.

Pull! They are levers! Pull! They're so clever!

These machines are great.

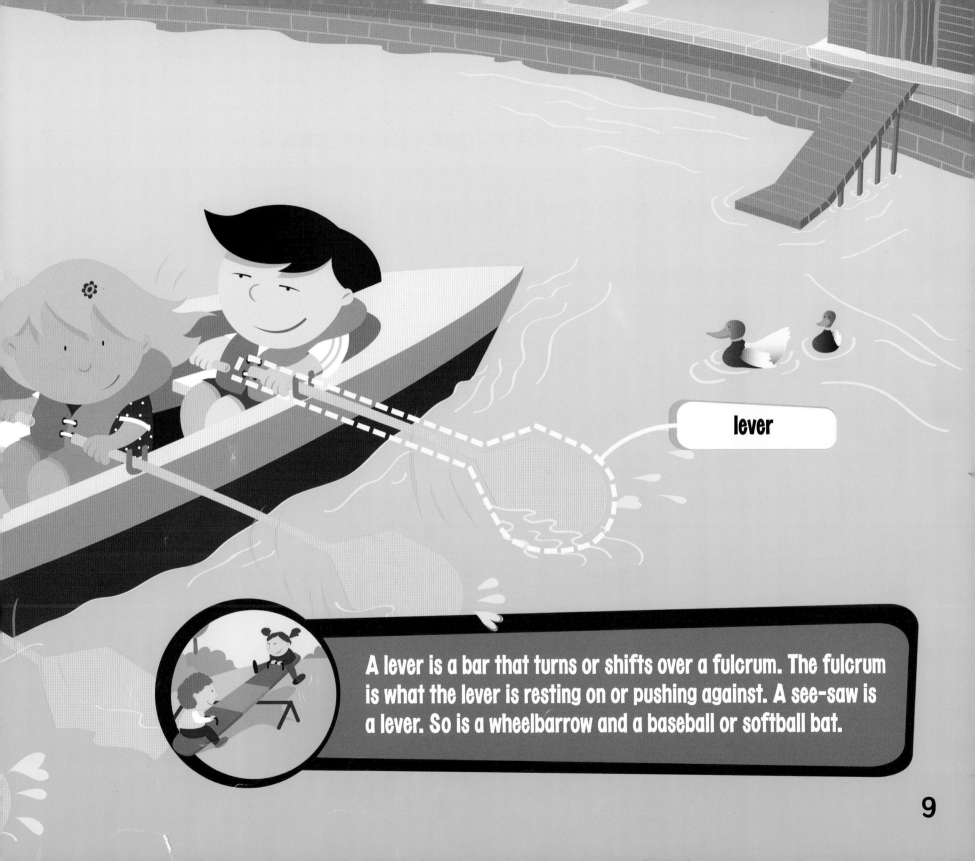

lever

A lever is a bar that turns or shifts over a fulcrum. The fulcrum is what the lever is resting on or pushing against. A see-saw is a lever. So is a wheelbarrow and a baseball or softball bat.

Can we build a fire and roast some snacks?

First we need a log and then an axe.

Bam! Sink the edge in! Slam! Sink the wedge in!

Give that wood some whacks!

A wedge is something that has a wide end and a narrow end. It can separate things and hold them in place. A doorstop is a wedge.

wedge

13

Do you know a crane contains a wheel,

Raises heavy objects made of steel?

Lift! Use the cable! Lift! Keep it stable!

Pulleys are ideal.

14

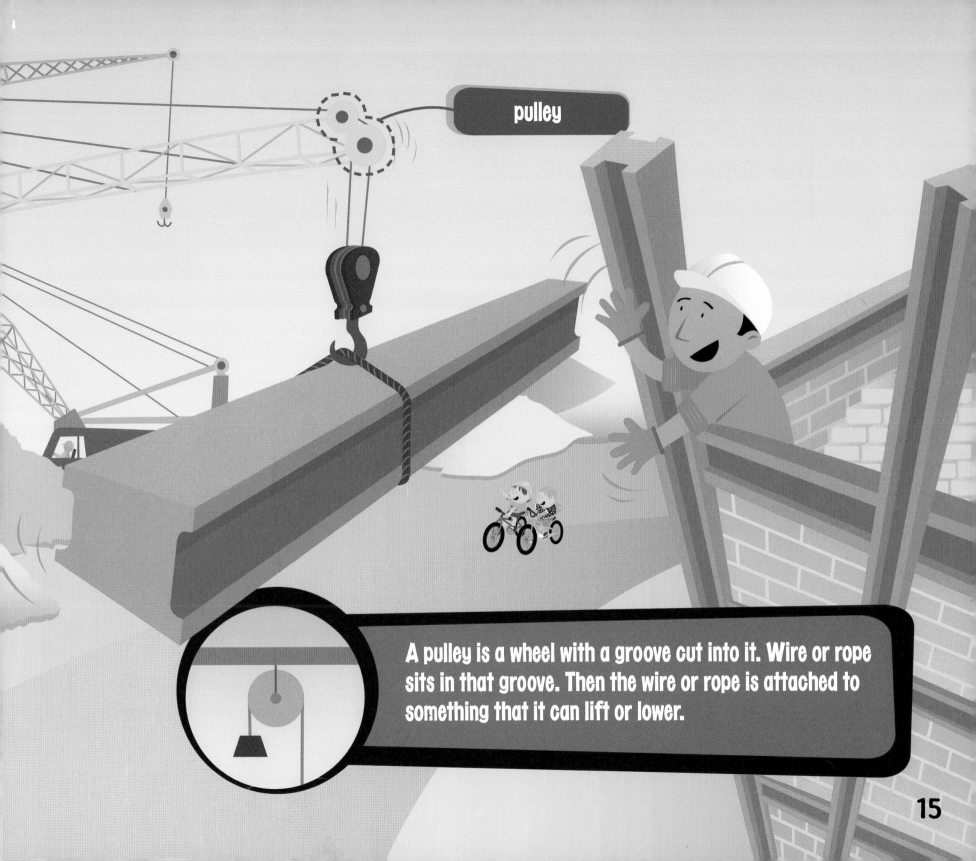

pulley

A pulley is a wheel with a groove cut into it. Wire or rope sits in that groove. Then the wire or rope is attached to something that it can lift or lower.

If a couple nails or glue won't do,

Take the time to learn to turn a screw.

Twist! See the groove! Twist! Make it move!

See what it can do.

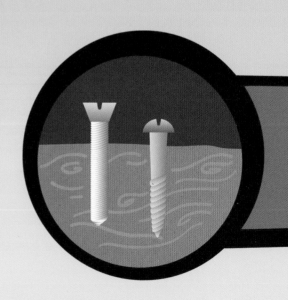

A screw is a sloping surface that winds around a bar, or shaft. It fastens or moves things. A screwdriver is a tool used to turn screws.

18

screw

19

These are things that help us work and play.

If you need to move things, they're the way.

Work! Use machines! Work! They're routine!

Use them every day.

OPEN

21

Move It! Work It!

Lift-ing the pi-ano is a great big pa-in.

It will give your back a great big stra-in.

Roll, yes it wi-ll! Roll, up the hi-ll!

Use an in-clined plane.

2. Do you ride a bike to your friend's each day?
Pedal place to place without delay?
Go, wheel and axle! Go, wheel and axle!
Take me far away.

3. When you row a rowboat on the lake,
Pairs of wooden oars are what you take.
Pull! They are levers! Pull! They're so clever!
These machines are great.

4. Can we build a fire and roast some snacks?
First we need a log and then an axe.
Bam! Sink the edge in! Slam! Sink the wedge in!
Give that wood some whacks!

5. Do you know a crane contains a wheel,
Raises heavy objects made of steel?
Lift! Use the cable! Lift! Keep it stable!
Pulleys are ideal.

6. If a couple nails or glue won't do,
Take the time to learn to turn a screw.
Twist! See the groove! Twist! Make it move!
See what it can do.

7. These are things that help us work and play.
If you need to move things, they're the way.
Work! Use machines! Work! They're routine!
Use them every day.

The audio file for this book is available for download at:
http://www.capstonekids.com/sciencesongs.html

Did You Know?

Simple machines make work easier. When you use them, you spend less energy to do the same amount of work. But it takes more time to do the work. The easier a job is to do, the longer it takes.

Simple machines are all around you. A wheelchair ramp is an example of an inclined plane. A Ferris wheel is a kind of wheel and axle. The spiral in a washing machine is a screw.

Even parts of your body act as simple machines. Your front teeth are wedges. When you take a bite out of a carrot, your teeth split it apart.

Big machines, such as cars or trains, are actually many small simple machines working together.

When machines don't work well, they create friction. Friction is the force that tries to stop movement.

Glossary

axle–a bar on which a wheel turns

fasten–to attach two things to each other

force–energy or strength

inclined–sloped

plane–a flat surface

routine–easy

stable–not easily moved

23

To Learn More

More Books to Read

Fowler, Allan. *Simple Machines.* New York: Children's Press, 2001.

Thales, Sharon. *Wheels and Axles to the Rescue.* Mankato, Minn.: Capstone Press, 2007.

Thompson, Gare. *Lever, Screw, and Inclined Plane: The Power of Simple Machines.* Washington, D.C.: National Geographic, 2006.

Index

On the Web

FactHound offers a safe, fun way to find educator-approved Internet sites related to this book.

Here's what you do:

1. Visit *www.facthound.com*
2. Choose your grade level.
3. Begin your search.

This book's ID number is 9781404852990

Look for all of the books in the Science Songs series:

♪ Are You Living?
A Song About Living and Nonliving Things

♪ From Beginning to End:
A Song About Life Cycles

♪ Home on the Earth:
A Song About Earth's Layers

♪ Move It! Work It!
A Song About Simple Machines